Teacher Affirmations

BURNABY BOOKS

Teacher Affirmations Book 1
Copyright © 2020 by David Seale

Published by Burnaby Books, an imprint of Burnaby, LLC

Burnaby titles may be purchased in bulk for educational, business, fund-raising or sales promotional use. For information please see www.burnabybooks.com.

Seale, David, 1969 –
Teacher Affirmations (#1) / by David Seale
    1.   Education, 2. Inspirational

Library of Congress Control Number: Pending
ISBN: 978-0-9796988-5-9

This book was printed in the United States of America.
1.0

Teacher Affirmations

Because You Have the Most Important Job
in the World

by

David Seale

No. 1

You really do....

ACKNOWLEDGEMENTS

While I may have written, recorded, and uploaded the podcast episodes that follow, no one does anything meaningful in isolation. My full and heartfelt thanks to all of the teachers, students, and administrators with whom I have worked. Thanks to the teachers I had when I was a student, from pre-school to graduate school. Every one of them made some type of difference and have provided knowledge, influence, experience, and inspiration, whether my experiences came from those who guided me in public school, college, or graduate school, or were colleagues in Tuscaloosa, Tarrant, Clanton, Jemison, Pelham, Birmingham City, or Mountain Brook, I thank all of them for having some type of impact that has helped guide me in this profession.

Thanks to the thousands of students I have taught or led; they are the reason, the Why, and I am eternally grateful.

Much appreciation to my longtime friend, partner in crime, and writing advisor, Richard Murff, who said, "A book full of podcast episodes? Let's do it!"

Finally, sincere gratitude to my family for the support, not just for this book and the podcast, but throughout my career's ups and downs. You make the difference. Always.

This book is dedicated to every person who has made the noble choice to impact the future by becoming a teacher.

Why do a podcast for educators, more specifically teachers? Well, like teaching, it's not for the money, because I don't make any from the podcast. It's not for the fame, because there are no educators on the cover of *Rolling Stone*, hanging with Ryan Reynolds, or presenting at the CMAs. It's not a project that is working towards a doctorate, because, at this stage in my career, I am less interested about any letters in front of my name and more interested in what I leave behind.

No, I created Teacher Affirmations because in the past few years, I have seen an unsettling trend amongst educators: early burnout and professional fatigue, in teachers way too young to feel that way as well as in veterans who have so much left to give. The increase in paperwork, duties, and stress combined with a decrease in validation and support are leading excellent and essential educators to leave the profession, and right now, the nation as a whole is suffering from a deficit of quality teachers.

The mission of the podcast is to validate and elevate the profession of teaching and education, providing words of inspiration, ideas for student growth, advice from leading education scholars, tricks of the trade, and maybe even a much needed laugh or two. We have the most important job in the world, and what is certainly one of the most difficult, especially in our current climate, and the role of the teacher at all levels has never been more crucial. To that end, I try to provide a three to five minute slice of encouragement and honesty that will hopefully bring some positivity to a teacher's day, week, year, and hopefully professional outlook.

And the mission of this collection of Teacher Affirmations episodes is to provide those same slices in book form. Something to pick up for a quick dose of momentum, a high five on Friday afternoon, or a Monday morning dash of hope in your coffee cup to get you going for the awesome work you do. The selections are organized loosely by theme, not the order in which they appeared on the podcast, and edits have been made to make them more reader-friendly.

Enjoy!

INSPIRATION

Education is the most powerful weapon which you can use to change the world.

- Nelson Mandela

YOU HAVE THE MOST IMPORTANT JOB

Education is an enigma as a profession. It is clear that the job is important, and ask any parent if it matters how good their child's teacher is, and they will have plenty to say in the affirmative. But when it comes to national respect, the tired, hackneyed phrase, "Those who can't do, teach" still seems to occupy a place in the backs of many minds, even if it is not stated outright as much as it once was. And when it comes to financial support, either in pay, resources, teacher units, or updated buildings, education is right there with the arts in not getting enough, and that is a symbolic gesture of how some feel about the importance of what we do.

But we didn't get into this profession to win popularity contests or be voted class favorite. We didn't get into it for the pay, and we certainly don't do it for all the accolades we receive. Even if we have to rediscover it at times, we know our Why. WE

13

know our vital role, even if we sometimes lose touch with it and even if those outside the profession never really understand.

It can be tough, however. And national statistics are showing that teaching is not the profession it used to be. There is a teacher shortage in our country, and far too many students in low-income school districts are in classrooms without highly qualified or certified teachers because those positions cannot be filled, especially in science and math. Special education and even elementary, where there used to be a surfeit, are now seeing unfilled openings, and the burnout rate for new teachers is also higher than ever. According to a 2015 report by Gray and Taie, 17% of all new teachers leave the profession in the first five years.

The reasons for all of these stats fill numerous books, studies, and Ted Talks, so I won't go into them here. What I want to do is make sure you remember that you truly are important, now more than ever. With shortages and burnout, our children need us more than ever. With the possibility of subpar education for some of our kids, turning up our own efforts to 11 is vital. We work with individuals, with people. And while researchers and policy makers love to put things into nice, neat numbers, when it comes down to it, education is a business of humans, of the future. A statistic or number cannot fully define the face of a child yearning to learn, of the pride of walking across a graduation stage, of receiving a college acceptance letter, of turning a C into an A, of a spelling bee, of a science fair, of a band competition, of the first day of kindergarten, of a holiday program, of a homecoming parade. The qualitative aspects of our work far outweigh the quantitative, so ignore the stats, ignore the numbers, ignore the uneducated opinions of those whose only experience in a school is that they once attended one decades ago. Don't let a tough day, inconsiderate parent email, a child's bad mood, or an administrator's surprise requirement dissuade you from doing this noble work.

You are doing what you were born to do, and you do it well. We need you, and more essentially, the kids need you. Every single one of them.

How Do You Eat a Whale?

Education can be overwhelming. In fact, I am sure that you are partly reading this chapter right now, but also partly thinking of things you need to get done at school. And how many times have you done that when your spouse or significant other is telling you about his or her day? When your own child is going on about soccer practice? Our minds are constantly trying to negotiate what is happening now with what needs to happen later. And with so many demands on a teacher in today's school culture, it's no wonder the rates of teacher burnout are high and retention low. So much of that is the overwhelming feeling that there is simply too much to do: grading, paperwork, responding to school and parent emails, planning, data collection, and the small requests from 100 people that add up to a lot of stress.

I coached a 4th grade community league basketball team last winter, and in the first round of the playoffs, we were down by 12 points at the start of the 4th quarter. The overwhelming belief that the deficit was too large to overcome was starting to creep into the minds of my guys, and they were visibly frustrated, so right before the start of the 4th quarter, when they were expecting an awesome fire-up speech from the coach, I simply asked, "How do you eat a whale?" Understandably, they looked at me like I was full-on crazy, but I repeated it: "How do you eat a whale?" They shrugged, and I said, "One bite at a time. Don't look at the scoreboard and think that we need to score 12; focus on each time we get the ball and think, 'we need to get two'. And soon, we won't need 12, we'll need 10, then eight, and so on."

With your job, don't try to eat the whale in one bite, and don't stare at the whale lamenting the impossibility of consuming it. Create bite-size goals for yourself and nibble away. Even if you are, for example, doing all of your math test grading in one evening, divide the tests up into small goals, and watch as you climb each small step. Soon, you're done with that bite, and it's time to move on to another. And give yourself some small rewards after each small goal is accomplished. You'll get more done than you realize!

Incidentally, my team won that game, and wound up winning the championship, and I am sure it was all due to their coach's fantastic "whale speech". Seriously, we won that game because my kids didn't get caught up in the anxiety of a seemingly insurmountable task, and instead took each basket one at a time. And that victory made them believe that they could clear any obstacle. You do the same, and watch as your efficiency grows as your to-do list shrinks. *Bon appetit*!

FAVORITE TEACHER

I want you to do something right now: I want you to think back to your school days, and I want you to think about your two or three favorite teachers. Maybe you already have your favorite in mind. But look back on your days in K-12 and try to select in your mind your two or three favorites.

Now choose one, and I want you to think about what made her or him your favorite then, and what still makes you view him or her as your favorite even today. Reflect on that for a few minutes, and if you want to list a few attributes, please do.

What are some of the attributes that lead you to your choice? What did she possess that set her apart from the dozens of teachers who entered and walked through your life? I have a feeling that the person you chose was not the easiest teacher you had, nor was he the most difficult. I doubt your favorite was all work and no play, nor all play and no work.

19

Chances are, your favorite possessed a combination of attributes: smart, kind, approachable, innovative, engaging. She probably challenged you to be better than you thought you could be, had high expectations and gave you the tools to reach them. You probably remember looking forward to going to his class because your favorite teacher made learning fun and genuine. Now think to yourself, how many of these traits do you possess? Do you strive to emulate these characteristics? I'm sure you do, even without consciously thinking about it.

Here's the kicker: it is now years later, and you are STILL influenced by this teacher, you still recognize her as positively impacting your life. That is the power of an excellent teacher. There are students in your classroom right now who, if asked years from now which teachers made the biggest difference, will name you. You have the opportunity and responsibility that goes with this power. It is great, it is impacting. It is real. And every day begins with a new chance to be that everlasting light. Be it, do it!

RECLAIMING YOUR WHY

I know it seems ridiculous to think about, but at times we lose sight of why we went into education. But in reality, the demands on teachers, the stress, the day-to-day grind can put us into a rut where we can lose touch with our Why. We are so consumed with what we have due today, tomorrow, next week. We have deadlines and expectations, most of which are imposed by others on us, and we can get wrapped up in those stresses. Which is why it is important to reclaim your Why at certain points in the year.

Here are some ways to do that. This is great to do at the beginning of the year to get inspired, but even more impactful when returning from December break, when burnout is starting to rear its ugly head. Most of this is from Simon Sinek's book *Start With Why*, and if you have never read it, I highly recommend it.

* First, ask yourself: Why did you go into this profession?

* Remind yourself that it must go beyond simply paying bills, benefits, or "because my mom was a teacher". And it needs to be deeper than "I love children". If that were the case, you could work in a day care. Why did you choose to be a teacher? Remember, if you don't know your Why, your kids definitely will not.

* When you get the chance, write down what can get in the way of staying true to your Why, and what you can do to stay focused on it. Maybe it's a mantra, maybe a new habit that refocuses yourself on the Why.

Also, when you get the time, the Ted Talk from Simon Sinek on You Tube is very worth it, and shows how from both a business and leadership perspective, knowing your why and leading with that engenders trust and belief from others, in our case, students.

There is no shame in being super-focused on creating fabulous learning opportunities for students. But it would be a shame if you found yourself uninspired because you had lost touch with what inspired you to touch lives in the first place. It's in you, always. Just bring it back.

REFRAMING YOUR WHY

I keep a framed 8x10 picture of Ernest Hemingway in my office, and have since I was still teaching high school English. While I appreciate his work, enjoyed teaching *A Farewell To Arms*, and usually read *Old Man and the Sea* once a year, I don't have the picture because I think Hemingway is history's greatest writer, nor is he even my favorite. The picture was actually given to me by a former colleague and means more than just a friendly professional gift. A lot more.

This former colleague was a co-worker, and at the time I joined that school's English department, she had been teaching 10th grade world literature for 30 years. At one time, she had been an all-star, but at the point we worked together, she had gotten to the point where many of her literary lectures were recorded, and she merely played them while she graded papers. Her tests were the same ones she had given for years, and her assignments were laminated so they could be re-used annually. She had what could be considered an unusual attachment to Hemingway and taught *Old Man and the Sea* every year, as she had in the late 60's. She had become the stereotypical old teacher phoning it in. And because she had been there so long, no one would say anything to her. Who is going to challenge a legend?

Luckily, the state department of education inadvertently forced the issue. A few years later, the state English curriculum changed so that 10th grade English became the first half of American Lit, with 11th grade becoming just 20th century American Lit. We all thought this would be the end of her career, that after 30+ years, she'd go to the house before she'd change what she was teaching. After all, she couldn't use her laminated lessons or pre-recorded lectures anymore. The only other option was for her to start over, and surely, she wasn't going to do that, right?

But that is exactly what she did. She realized that she wasn't ready to retire, she still had a fire in her. She started working that summer with younger teachers to create their curriculum guide, lessons, and reading lists. She offered her own expertise, but mainly opened herself to learn from other colleagues. One day, she came by my classroom with an armful of posters and binders. "David, I've been teaching Papa for a long time, but won't be this year, so I'm giving you my Hemingway stuff since you'll be teaching him. Give him a good home." And I did, because her reclaiming of her Why lit a fire in me as well.

It still does when I glance at that framed picture, reminding me that any teacher can lose his/her way, but every teacher can rediscover it, and create positive impact in the lives of students. And when I get overwhelmed, that picture gets me back on track as well.

REFLECT WHAT YOU EXPECT

There is a popular mantra in education, especially amongst administrators, that goes like this: "Inspect what you expect." In other words, if you have expectations of students, of their work, or their proficiency, and you have communicated these expectations, you have to inspect to make sure the effort, the work, and results show mastery of these expectations, and if they don't, make alterations in your plans to ensure these expectations are met. How many times have we had or seen teachers who give work, expect completion and certain skills, but then never follow up to make sure achievement happens? So, yes, it is important to inspect what we expect, to follow through on what is important.

But let's take the catchy, rhyming mantra-making a step further. We may inspect what we expect, but do we REFLECT what we expect? What kind of example do we set? Are we as true in our actions as we are in our words? I work with administrators all the time and am fascinated by how many will complain about teacher tardiness but then come to work themselves as the first bell is ringing. If you expect it, reflect it! Model it, walk the walk, back up the talk. In your classroom, do you expect punctual, high quality work? Then make sure you are modeling that expectation in yourself. Do you stress respectful behavior towards all in your room? Then refrain from anything that might be deemed disrespectful to others: sarcasm, put downs, gossip, negative remarks about co-workers. Do you demand punctuality? Then be on time, and show that everyone's time is valuable, including yours.

Besides avoiding hypocrisy, which students of all ages see through like plastic wrap, you also give importance to your expectations. Even small things, like showing kids you read for pleasure, that you go to museums, that you balance your own checkbook, that you use the knowledge you have - all of these seemingly small acts have lasting impact. Students see the WHY in what they are doing, and you are modeling for students the qualities of conviction and integrity, things not all students see in their other adult influences. Yes, inspect what you expect, but reflect it, too!

SELF-CARE

We've talked about your Why, why did you become a teacher, where is your teaching passion? While not everyone will have the same answer to the Why question, I would imagine it is rooted in all of us in a deep sense of service we all feel and in which we all believe. You chose to teach because you believe that you are part of a noble profession, one that gives back not just to a community but to generations. You are a part of something bigger than yourself that will make this world a better place.

I truly hope you feel that way, and I believe you do. There is a slight flip-side to that conviction, however. People like us who choose a service profession, one that does not pay what a private sector job would pay, and one that is stressful and intense at times, do so because we want to give to others more than to ourselves, and that is wonderful and essential and part of why you are so important.

But because we do have servant's hearts, we are all guilty of sacrificing ourselves: our health, our families, our energy, our growth. And we need to talk about why it's important to be able to shift the focus to self-care when we need it.

In 2004, I was still teaching high school English and coaching a nationally competitive debate program. There is no doubt that I spent a lot of time after hours at work; in fact, my debate coaching duties usually had me with students 10-15 weekends a year competing all over the country - Boston, Honolulu, Portland, Chicago, Atlanta, Nashville, Dallas, San Francisco - everywhere. In May of that year, I had double hernia surgery (note to self - do not pick up any more lawnmowers and put them in your car), and if you know anything about the surgery, the recovery is 7-10 days, very painful, but then once it's over, you can get back into action pretty quickly. Well, I tried to go back to school too soon, and my first day back, that afternoon during my prep period, I was standing in my doorway, feeling faint, hurting pretty bad. One of the baseball coaches and intervention teachers, Mr. Honeycutt, walked by on his way to the fields, stopped, looked at me and said, "David, you don't look so good."

I replied, "I don't feel so good."

He said, "Why don't you go home, come back when you're healed."

I said, "But Tony, I have exams coming up I need to get kids ready for, I have the national debate tournament in a few weeks we have to prepare for, I just have too much to do."

Tony looked at me and said, "David, if you die, they'll find someone to teach English. You have to take care of yourself." And as blunt as that was, he was right. So I stayed home two more days to recover, and came back sound as a pound.

I will forever value that conversation because it is a reminder that great teachers have a tendency to sacrifice a lot of themselves for their jobs, and it's easy to do so, even to the point of neglected health, because we can always look in the mirror and justify it by saying, "It's for the kids." It is, but also remember this: if you are too exhausted, stressed, or physically or emotionally unhealthy, are you giving the kids your best? You may be staying late at work, giving up your own free time for the sake of your job, but missing exercise and sleep, or meaningful moments with family or friends, or healthy meals and spiritual growth. The tradeoff isn't equitable. Don't let the job become your life. Sure, there are times we need to stay late, grade papers on weekends, plan in the evenings after dinner. But don't let that keep you from taking care of yourself. We have the most important job, but we can't do it if we are not at our best. Balance it out, and see to it that you give yourself some TLC.

BLOOMING IN ANY GARDEN

Many years ago, I was the principal in a 3-5 school with about 725 students. The job was intense, and there were several mountains to climb, but I couldn't ask for better kids, and the majority of the staff was passionate about teaching and loved children. Moreover, I had an exceptional front office staff. But a new superintendent was elected in the winter of the year. I have opinions on elected school officials, but I will save those for my memoirs. Suffice it to say that appeasing voters and improving instruction come from very different perspectives. And since one of his big supporters wanted my job, the new superintendent moved me from a job I really liked to being the site administrator at the system's alternative school. Not an upgrade. And because there had never been an administrator on site at that facility, there was some mild chaos to address.

I was furious and so disappointed. I felt like I was doing good work at the elementary school, that progress was happening. Parents, staff members, students alike were upset. But there was nothing I could do.

Actually, I had a few choices. I could quit. I could phone it in. I could use a bunch of the 80 sick days I had accrued. I could get a lawyer, I suppose, and try to fight my reassignment. But none of those options seemed to be logical, practical, or positive. I really just had one choice that was positive, and that was to go to the alternative school and get down to business. Which is what I did. When I arrived in April, twelve of the students there were on track to fail the grade and be yet another grade level behind. I worked them hard, arranged real support from the parent schools, made all of us accountable for their success, and by the end of the semester, everyone at the alternative school passed to the next grade.

The thing is, I didn't do anything any more spectacular than what teachers do every day in every school. I put the kids first and rolled up my sleeves. Did I get up every morning fired up about going to work. No. Let's be honest. There were days I cursed that reassignment, and because this is a family publication, I won't mention the words I had for the superintendent. But once I pulled up to the building and got out of my car, it wasn't about David anymore.

Teachers do that all the time. The point of my story is that we don't always get planted in the garden of our choice. Maybe it is a reassignment or not getting a job for which you interviewed. Maybe you asked to change grade levels but were denied. Maybe your favorite principal of all time took a new job in July and her replacement is her opposite and is driving you crazy. Maybe you got "that class" this year, or the board of education changed the curriculum....again. But you have been planted in a garden, and you have a choice. You can choose to bloom or to whither away. You can go from flower to fruit and share your growth with others, or you can deny them your potential. From personal experience, I can tell you that choosing to bloom reaps rewards for more than just the students.

At the end of that year, I was offered a principal's job in another system, and believing that to be more in line with my strengths, I took it. But I have never regretted my time at the alternative school because it showed me that we have the ability to make a difference, even if it is not exactly where we imagined we'd be. So wherever you are, bloom!

IMPACT

A teacher affects eternity; she can never tell where her influence stops.

– Henry B. Adams

WHAT IS BEST?

When I was still a classroom teacher and working on my administrative certification, I set up a meeting with my principal to ask some questions for my internship. When I arrived at our appointed time, he was finishing up a parent/student/teacher meeting, with all parties leaving his office, and when they had left, I leaned in and asked if I needed to come back at another time. He said, "No, come in and have a seat. I just need a minute to shift gears." He paused, and I could see the stress in his face.I have always admired him both as a leader and as a person; he is able to balance deep, genuine compassion with intelligent, critical problem solving. I still admire him, though I haven't worked with him in almost 15 years. That moment he said, "David, here is some advice: if you ever have a parent/ student/teacher meeting, and everyone walks out thinking they got what they wanted, you did something wrong. You either were not clear, made a promise you can't keep, or misunderstood a part of the problem. Inevitably, someone will walk away dissatisfied."

I asked, "So what do you do when they all want something different?"

He looked at me and said, "Whenever I have a problem and don't immediately feel the solution, I ask myself, 'What is best for the student?' And I act on the answer to that question. That way, no matter who feels slighted or frustrated with my decision, I know I can look in the mirror and know I did right by the child." He imparted several nuggets of wisdom in his time as my principal, but nothing as impacting as that.

As educators we are confronted with choices and decisions all the time, many of which include competing claims. In those instances, we can always turn to that advice and know the right choice. Obviously, there are certain times we have to comply no matter how we feel; you may not think starting school at 8am is the best time for kids to learn, but if the district says 8, school starts at 8. However, with other decisions, always use what is best for the students as your compass. Maybe your grade level team is ready to move to a new math standard, but you know your kids haven't mastered the current one; move on with your team or hang back? Maybe a parent thinks you should spend more time on math and less on reading. Maybe you have a choice to do intervention on a skill none of your kids seemed to master, or go outside for extra recess.

This advice can positively impact you as a parent as well, especially if you happened to be divorced; "I feel a certain emotion and want to take this action, but is that what is best for my child or children?" Let that question guide you. It removes emotion, conflict, and confusion. And in matters of the heart, removing the emotion is key to sound decision-making.

That doesn't mean every decision will become easy; it just makes the decision easier to support without regret.

SOMEBODY'S SOMEBODY

I have worked for some amazing educational leaders, but perhaps the best is the superintendent of the Birmingham City School System, Dr. Lisa Herring. Her daily actions are a master class on leadership, and she has guided a system that was temporarily under state supervision to an achieving urban school district. I could write a book on her, and one day I might, and you will most likely hear her name again if you hopefully continue to connect with Teacher Affirmations.

Before the start of one school year, she was addressing a huge room full of every administrator and central office employee in the system. She was talking about school culture, and said, and I am paraphrasing, "I want you to think of that special somebody in your life, that person who makes your world, your heart, your day light up every time you see them. That someone who brings meaning to your life. Think about that person. It could be your child, a parent, a spouse, a boyfriend or girlfriend. Picture them in your mind, your Somebody. Now, think about this: every child in our schools is Somebody's Somebody. Don't they deserved to be treated like Somebody?"

Wow. Every child is somebody's somebody. Every kid in your fourth period English lit block, every child in your kindergarten class, every player on your volleyball team, every student in your homeroom. Every one of them is somebody's somebody.

We all went into this profession with a love of learning and a love of children and a belief in their future, and we can't imagine ill ever befalling any of our students. But we do have those days or those long stretches of weeks where we feel burned out, out of gas, and out of patience. We always have in our hearts our purpose and our Why, but the stress and challenge of our jobs can sometimes get in the way. You're not a bad teacher or person for feeling that; you're human. But a way for you to get your true focus and priorities back is to remember that statement: every child is somebody's somebody. He or she is the light in somebody's world in the same way your somebody is for you.

Little Johnny who won't stop asking you questions is somebody's somebody. Big Charlie who hasn't said a kind word to you or anyone for that matter, all year, is somebody's somebody. Amber who never shows up to class on time and never has a pass is somebody's somebody. Jeremiah who always forgets to take his medication before running out the door to school is somebody's somebody. Bethany who could make all A's but refuses to turn in work or even try is somebody's somebody. Even Billy, the class bully; even David, the class clown; even Jenny, the class hypochondriac. All of them are somebody's somebody.

So when you think you may have lost your last bit of patience for the day, take a deep breath and a step back, and remember they are somebody.

BELIEF IN STUDENTS

I am a huge fan of the work by education researcher, John Hattie. Because I am skeptical of new teaching or pedagogical fads based on case studies or on the author's experience only, I appreciate Hattie's meta-study findings, where he actually culls through over 80,000 education studies to find the trends across time and the globe, to see what sorts of influences on student achievement have the most impact. In some cases, traditional approaches do not have data to back them up, whereas elements we might overlook have tremendous positive influence.

So, the most impacting influence on student achievement? Collective efficacy and high teacher estimate of student achievement. In other words: belief that all students can achieve, setting the bar high, and giving them the support to get there. This has more positive impact than any reading program, scheduling strategy, professional development, or textbook series. It starts with belief. Both in the classroom with the individual teacher as well as the collective faculty, a culture of high expectations and belief in the abilities of every student.

You can't control the whole staff (unless you're an administrator, in which case you may not control but can certainly influence the faculty as a whole), but you can control what you do and what you present in your own classroom.

A few ways to let your students know you believe in their ability to achieve:

* Create consistent and fair behavioral expectations and follow through

* As often as possible, have one-on-one conferences with students to discuss progress, and in this conference, be real about effort and your own support. How can this be changed to see better outcomes?

* Smile, always use a respectful tone, call students by name. Students need to see you treat them respectfully as individuals.

* Get to know each individual student's academic situation; what can you do to be equitable? Remember, equity and equality are not the same things. What one person needs may not be what everyone needs.
* When students fail to reach a goal, don't lower the expectation - raise your game and enthusiasm!

Remember, every student can learn, just maybe not on the same day in the same way as others. And you have the power to get each one on the path to success! This is a topic I truly believe in, so we will revisit it from time to time.

LASTING IMPACT THAT MATTERS

I'm going to tell a true story, and one that is somewhat personal, in that it involves people I know, so I know it's true. One of my closest friends, Richard, contacted me last week to tell me his older sister had passed away suddenly; she had gone in for some routine surgery, but developed a blood clot and passed quickly thereafter. Completely unexpected, entirely tragic, and left a husband and three sons without an irreplaceable piece of the family picture. A teacher at an all-boys private school in Memphis, she was only 52, with a lot left to give.

I was able to attend the funeral but not the visitation, so Richard told me about what occurred. What was supposed to be a two hour event lasted three, until the church director finally just had to close the doors. The mayor of Memphis was there, and according to the director, the attendance surpassed anything he could remember, even the services of city dignitaries and captains of industry. But here's the thing: Marie was not a buzzing socialite; she wasn't a mover or shaker in the Memphis financial, social, or charity scenes. She was a teacher, a mother, a wife, a sister, and daughter, who, according to her brother, had a handful of very close forever-friends, but that was about it. So the incredible crowd at her visitation was not filled with name-drop-worthy local celebrities. It was filled with family and friends, but mostly former students. Hundreds of them. Richard said that he spent two and half hours shaking the hands of former students, some still in school, others graduated, to the point where it became a blur. But they all communicated the same thing: she made a huge positive impact in their lives, an impact I don't think Marie could have predicted, but one that is clearly massive in its depth and breadth. And in case you are wondering, the mayor was there because Marie taught his sons, and he truly appreciated her impact as well. Richard told me that, knowing his sister, she would be prouder of her students paying tribute than the mayor, that seeing her impact would have been the real satisfaction. In his words, "They were her students, her boys. It was a massive comfort even if it is sad that we wait until someone is dead before we describe the impact on our lives."

There is an episode of the original Twilight Zone TV series where an elderly English teacher at a prep school is told that he will not be asked back after the winter holidays, so the school can make room for a younger teacher. He is heartbroken, and starts to wonder if the 50 years he dedicated to the profession and that school were worth it. He even contemplates suicide, but then hears school bells mysteriously ringing at night. He goes to his classroom, and it is filled with the ghosts of former students who had been killed in action during one of the two World Wars. And they all tell him how the wisdom he passed along to them helped them during times of fear, sorrow, and triumph, and he realizes he did make a difference. Thanks to the miracle of Netflix, you can watch it yourself, entitled "Changing of the Guard".

Obviously, we'll never have that supernatural experience. But both Marie's life and that episode show us something we must never forget: whether we can actually see it or feel it, even if we don't believe it, we have immeasurable impact on the lives of the children in our classrooms and schools. We may not even know the type of impact. It could be academic, social, or even emotional. In truth, we can never know the full scope of our positive influence. But it is there, it is powerful.

Richard asked me to share her story on this podcast, because, in his words, "If she got even one teacher to really put her back into it on a day they really didn't feel like it, if she could help them see why it matters, well... that would be better than the hundreds who showed up to say goodbye."

On a side note, Marie was an organ donor, so after her passing, her eyes were given to someone without sight. She provided true vision, both literally and figuratively, at a level higher than she could imagine. And you provide vision and guidance as well, so don't stop!

And rest in peace Marie Murff Duncan. May your dedication to others continue to make a difference.

CLIMATE

They may forget what you said but they will not forget how you made them feel.

– Carl Buechner

POWER OF POSITIVITY

We live in a world that is sometimes so driven by outcomes, that we take human connection for granted. Which is why something as simple as a smile or pleasant, unsolicited remark like "Have a great day", or "Thank you so much; that made a difference" seems to take us aback. Are we less cordial as a society as we used to be? I have opinions on that, but that's not the focus of this podcast. Suffice it to say, though, that positivity and random kindness are less the norm than they once were.

Which is why your opportunity to provide that to your students every day is so impacting. Simple things make a huge difference. And with some of our students, your positivity and kindness might be the only samples they get all day. Sad, but true, so let's give it to them!

Here are a few easy ways to bring the sunshine:

- Smile. Just smile. Smile when you greet them first thing, smile when you are handing out papers, smile when the fire alarm goes off.

- When greeting students, refer to them by name, and say something positive when you do, like "Good morning, Carlos. It's going to be a great day" or "You're going to achieve great things today."

- Compliment individual students on specific academic or behavioral achievements, no matter how small. "Allison, I appreciate you picking up that trash and throwing it away. A clean work environment is important to learning."

- Express pride in student achievement. Whether it is whole group or individual, students are uplifted when they know they have met the expectations of the teacher, and when they know you are pleased, it carries a lot of weight.

The amazing thing about positive words and actions is that they usually have just as much impact on you as they do on your students. When you express positivity, it does something to your own attitude, so that even if you are not feeling the positivity at first (and let's face it - we all have those days when we fake it until we make it), the more you give out, the better you feel.

REDUCING NEGATIVITY

Because you are the type of teacher who reads education books (and hopefully listens to education podcasts), you are also probably the type who attends professional development by choice, works well with colleagues, and finds joy not just in being a teacher but also becoming an even better one. You get worn out, and at times of the year, maybe even a little burned out, but it's temporary, and you can be brought back from that with reminders of why you became a teacher. The job is challenging and hard, but to you, it's rewarding beyond measure.

But let's face it: not all of our co-workers are in the same place or have the same perspectives or priorities. They are negative and critical, gossipy and prickly. They can be toxic to a work environment, and they can be so negative about the job, co-workers, students, and administrators, they make you wonder why they entered the profession. Or if they even like children. These folks always have a complaint but never a solution, and never seem to want to own any part of why something is not working well. They can dismantle a school culture, and tend to be outspoken and bully-like, so few people have the energy or courage to push back against them. Ignore them, and they'll go away, right? But they usually don't. While some of these Negative Nancys or Neds spend time counting the days to summer and/or retirement, others are going nowhere, so we're stuck with them.

Or are we? It's easy to get dragged down by these negative co-workers, but there are peaceful ways to address them and hopefully quell some of their toxic attitudes. I have used some of these strategies, and others are by Todd Whitaker from his book, *10 Minute In-Service*:

- Return negativity with the opposite. When he is talking negatively about a student, reply with, "I love that kid." There is no response to this. Or even, "He can be spirited; let's think of ways to re-focus his energy." Negative folks don't like solutions. Or even, "It's those kinds of students that made me become a teacher - I love those kids."

- When approached by gossip, say, "Love to chat, but I have so much to do."

- With any type of negative comment about policy or procedures, a response that usually shuts down this person is, "You make an interesting point. Let's see about setting up a meeting with our administrator to discuss some ways to solve this problem." Or, "How would you do it differently?" Remember, Negative Nancy is not interested in solutions because then there is nothing about which to complain.

Finally, when you are feeling discouragement creep in on your own disposition, do not allow Negative Nancy to draw it out of you. They are experts at seeing your negative thoughts and love to pretend to care as a sounding board. In reality, they will only feed that negative fire, and possibly tell others the content of your steam-blowing. So when they come to you and ask, "What's wrong?", just smile and say you're just a little worn out today, but you're looking forward to tomorrow.

Dealing with negative co-workers isn't easy, but when everyone around them refuses to allow their attitude to rain on the school parade, they will either cool off, find other negative outlets, or leave. You can't change them, but you can change how you deal with them. And who knows? Maybe you can relight

whatever fire there once was in their teacher heart.
Worth a try!

PEER OBSERVATIONS

Professional development and growth. The images and feelings that concept conjures up will be different for each reader. For some of you, an awesome workshop is a great way to recharge your teaching batteries, so your first thought was, "Those can be really good!" For others, that phrase brings to mind endless lectures and Powerpoints, maybe some obligatory sticky-note group work, and a day you could have been working in your classroom. I get it. I feel both ways. I have been a part of some truly game-changing professional development that helped me reframe my perspective on an element of instruction, where I was thankful for the knowledge, and I know it had impact when I took it back to school. On the other hand, I have been forced to attend PD that made me question my vocational choice, and I spent most of the time thinking of what physical pain I might endure if it meant getting to leave. I found no value in the workshop, and saved my colleagues the time of turning it around back at school. So that phrase doesn't guarantee any growth or benefits, nor does it guarantee a waste of time.

The truth is, growth is essential to being a great educator. Whether it is reading a professional book, attending a workshop, viewing a webcast, or going to a conference, finding new ways to hone your craft is vital. The trick for administrators is to create or locate professional learning opportunities that provide bang for the buck, don't feel like "another thing" or "the next thing", and can impact learning in practice, not just in theory. That is another knock on professional development, that it sounds great from the stage but can't translate into an actual classroom.

To that end, I have found that some of the best PD I could offer my staff was PD they created and shared with each other. If it was based at our school, came from our teachers, then it had a much better chance to positively impact the learning of our students. Every teacher has something to offer. But it doesn't have to be a traditional workshop or training. And it doesn't have to be something the school or system administrators require and implement. One particularly valuable bit of PD comes from right next door, so to speak.

Peer observations are a great way to learn new things, grow as a teacher, and improve and strengthen the collegial climate. But you can wreck that boat just as quickly as you can sail it, so before embarking, here are a few tips.

1. No surprises. Set it up with a colleague in advance.

2. Have an idea of what it is you want to learn and find a teacher who is well-known for being strong in that area. Simply wandering into a classroom without focus might be a waste of time.

3. First try to get your grade-level or department on board as a whole so you can all be doing it. And if so, you may be able to get your principal to set it up to where you get credit hours.

4. After the observation, send an email to the teacher you observed. First, thank her, then name one awesome thing you observed, and one thing you think you will implement into your own teaching or classroom. This makes the whole process a positive

one. You get valuable learning, and your co-worker gets valuable validation. Resist the temptation to give advice; first, it's not really your job, and it's not really the point. And it's a quick way to keep that opportunity from happening again.

Give it a try! Complacency is the enemy of success, and you can always improve, even if you don't think anything is broken. And peer observations sure beat another boring workshop.

LEAST FAVORITE TEACHER

Several chapters earlier, I asked you to think about your favorite teacher ever, and to recall all of those attributes that person possessed that made her your favorite teacher. I'm sure you had no problem coming up with an inspirational former teacher, and chances are, that person continues to inspire you.

It is amazing how much impact we have as educators. Even things we consider small and routine could have massive impact in the day, year, life of a child. So we take pause to reflect upon and appreciate those educators who made the positive difference.

But something else to consider is the awesome responsibility of that influence. Because just as we have the power to positively impact a child's life, we also have the power to negatively impact a child. This is usually done without malice or intent, and in most cases, a result of a moment of frustration, stress, or weakness. Other times, it is poor judgement or inexperience. But only in rare instances is a professional educator truly trying to negatively affect a child with intent. In the end, it doesn't matter - damage can be done.

So I want you to take a moment to recall your least favorite teacher. Just a moment. Think about why this person is your least favorite. Was there a particular incident that affected you? Or maybe it was his attitude? Maybe the work wasn't challenging and the next year, you struggled because of lack of preparation? How did this teacher make you feel about yourself? Chances are, you are recalling some uncomfortable or maybe painful memories, and I apologize if this exercise has brought in a dark cloud. I present at a lot of workshops and will ask a group to do this very exercise, and it is amazing how much that least favorite teacher impacts the adults in the room. Some actually get emotional sharing with the group. But I wanted to illustrate in another way not only how important our jobs are, but also the incredible influence we have.

I'm sure you don't exhibit any of the characteristics of your least favorite teacher. But do you work with someone who does? If so, are there ways you can help this colleague trend upward, or maybe go to an administrator and express your concern? You don't want to feel like a snitch, but think about this: research shows that one bad year with a bad teacher can put a child two years behind in their learning. No child deserves that.

I was an advanced math student until a bad junior high math teacher who refused to meet with me for after or before school help because, in her words, "I don't have time for you, David, now or ever." Ouch. Struggled with math for the next three years. My own child had a very subpar 1st grade teacher, and consequently found reading so distasteful that she was in 3rd grade before she began to read for pleasure. And I'm sure you can fill in the blank with your own bad teacher experience. Bottom line: what we do is too vital to be done poorly. Never forget your impact and your potential to influence the lives of young people. You make the difference!

CLASSROOM

Education is not the filling of a pail but the lighting of a fire.

- William Butler Yeats

PROUD OF MY SCHOOL

One of my brothers shares with me a fondness for stage acting. In fact, even though we are six years apart, we have had the opportunity to be cast together in a couple of plays, and the gift to be able share that has been terrific. To be honest, while I am not bad, my brother is fantastic. He appeared in a production in August, and it was such a good show, and he was so spectacular in it, that I forgot for a while that I was related to him; the characters and action had become so riveting that I no longer saw him as my brother, but as his character. And when the show was over, I felt such pride that I was related to the star of the show, that when people realized I was his brother, they seemed to revere me just a little, just by association. I was so incredibly proud of him, and sharing a last name with him made me feel special. Needless to say, I was the first to stand for the ovation, and I couldn't wait to tell others about the show.

I'm sure we have all had such an experience. Maybe it is pride in a child's accomplishments, or a former student, spouse or family member. Heck, I get excited when I'm watching a sporting event and a player is recognized as being from my hometown or my alma mater. In fact, using that example, if I am casually watching a game, my engagement in the action is heightened when I feel connected to some elevated greatness on the field or court, more so than if I didn't know of that connection. I am certainly not suiting up and playing, and if that player's team wins the Super Bowl, David's not getting a ring. But that connection to greatness gives me pride and increases my engagement. I care more about the outcome.

Todd Whitaker, in his book *Ten Minute Inservice*, suggests listing reasons why you are proud of your school as a way to fight negativity, or to give yourself a lift when you might be feeling negative. As he states, it seems far easier to point out faults than successes. I'm no psychologist, but I think that may go back to our innate tendency to want to fix things, to make things better, and so we may naturally notice what needs fixing before what is going well. Teachers and educators in general want to make things better, solve problems, so we are prone to notice the scars and not the beauty marks. You're welcome, and I won't even charge you for today's session. But seriously, all "fixers" or natural helpers have that radar. Sometimes, though, we need to see the positive. And listing reasons to be proud of your school is a great way to do that.

I would like to take that a step further. Your students need that positivity as well. So take your school pride and expose your class or classes to it. Create space on a bulletin board or outside your classroom door to post evidence of things about which to be proud in your school. It could be school, group, or sports achievements; it could be individual accolades; it could be things school students have been recognized for in the community. Maybe your school was recognized for higher achievement data; maybe the debate team won a tournament out of state; maybe the football team made the playoffs; maybe one of the students at the school was celebrated in the local paper for an Eagle scout project; maybe an alum achieved something noteworthy; maybe an alum is historically significant. But celebrate them and connect your kids to school pride. Like in the example I used earlier about being more engaged in an otherwise ordinary sporting event when I see I have a personal connection to a player, increasing school pride within individual students makes them more engaged in the actual school experience. School pride has been shown to increase attendance and parental involvement, so don't ignore this natural positive resource. Tap into it for a boost in overall morale and engagement.

THE ROOT OF MISBEHAVIOR

I know every single person reading this book has the perfect classroom of students, that there are never any behavior problems and that your classroom management system is so airtight that misbehavior is like the Yeti: you've heard stories, but because you've never seen it, it probably doesn't exist.

Then you wake up, because such a classroom is a dream, not reality. Even in the most well-managed classrooms, there are discipline issues. The key, though, is not to look at the incident as a problem, but as a symptom.

Student behavior specialist Brian Mendler reminds us that a moment of misbehavior is really the symptom of a bigger problem, and dealing with just the symptom and not the root cause will never cure the misbehavior. An analogy: a sore throat is a symptom of the regular sinus infections I get, but if all I do is take a throat lozenge, the real infection still exists, even if my throat feels temporarily better.

Let's say Jimmy is late to class Monday morning, and when he arrives, he is clearly in a poor mood. You say, "Jimmy, you're late. Do you have a pass?", and Jimmy then proceeds to yell back at you, raising his voice. You ask him to please lower his tone, and he gets even more belligerent. The infraction here, along with being tardy, is defiance and disrespect, and please don't misunderstand me here: the infraction must be dealt with. But defiance and disrespect are not the problem; they are symptoms of a deeper problem. Maybe Jimmy's mom didn't come home last night; maybe Jimmy's girlfriend just broke up with him; maybe Jimmy had an argument with his brother on the way to school; maybe Jimmy didn't have a meal all weekend and he missed breakfast at school. Yes, deal with the infraction, but then, get to the root of the real problem. Discuss this with Jimmy (when he has had a chance to calm down), and talk about how to approach the situation better the next time, that defiance and disrespect won't be tolerated regardless, so let's figure out a better way to fix the response. Is there anything I can do to help with the larger problem? Do you need to see the school counselor or principal?

The payoffs here are huge, the largest being the trust and relationship building that happens when you don't merely view Jimmy's actions as isolated problems but view Jimmy as a human with needs. Plus, you diffuse the root problem, which makes the probability of the symptoms occurring very slim. When you do this, all of the Jimmys in your class will see that you respect them as individuals, and this respect will come back to you all year.

INSTRUCTIONAL

All students can learn and succeed, but not in the same way and not in the same day.

– William G. Spady

REACH BELOW, TAKE THEM HIGH

I was in a meeting at the beginning of the school year with a middle school principal, his assistant principal, and several curriculum coordinators from the central office, and we were discussing how we could best support the school at the start of the semester. One of the principal's main concerns is one that teachers and administrators across the country feel, that teachers, because so many students are below grade level, are teaching lower grade material, watered down standards, or low rigor lessons. And instead of increasing the rigor, these teachers are staying low so that the students are successful, since they cannot do grade-level work right now. Why set them up for failure?

In the meeting, we then discussed the importance of meeting students where they are, and that good teaching differentiates for varying student learning levels and abilities. But the problem still remained, that once the teachers are meeting students where they are, they are keeping them there. The progression of rigor wasn't happening. Furthermore, students above grade level weren't being challenged at all, so everyone was staying low.

The ELA curriculum coordinator then gave this analogy. I'm paraphrasing, but she said, "If I join a gym because I have a goal to bench press 100 pounds, at my current level, my personal trainer needs to start me off with some 5 pound dumbbells. If he starts me off at 100, I will not be able to do it, and no amount of straining to lift it is going to make it happen. And I would probably just give up. So I would need to start where I am. But if he keeps me at 5 pound dumbbells, I will never reach my goal. He will need to gradually increase weight, and there will be times when I will think I can't do it, and other times I will be sore the next morning, but I am getting stronger, especially with his support. And soon, I'll be able to bench press 100 pounds."   I love that analogy, because it's something with which we can all identify. We have all set goals to be better, stronger, smarter, or set goals to learn a new skill, to save money for a trip, to lose weight. I know people who have trained to run a 10K, but they certainly didn't start by running ten kilometers. Instead, they gradually built strength and stamina.

The same applies to our students. We meet them where they are, but if we do not raise them up, we are doing them a disservice. Will an increase in rigor hurt, so to speak? Definitely, but when they start to see their own growth in skills and stamina, they will stick with it. If I am trying to lose a few pounds, the increase in exercise and decrease in ice cream and adult beverages may be hard to do at first, but when I can tell when I put on a pair of dress pants that they fit better and feel more comfortable, and when I see the evidence (or data) when I step on the scale, I am more inclined to continue to work at it because I am seeing success.

And there is a good chance that failure at academic growth in the past has been a factor in motivation for some students to want to learn. They were given work that was the equivalent of a 10K, couldn't do it, and then said, to heck with it. But when you meet them where they are and help them actually grow, with support and encouragement, they will see it and surprise you with how much more they want to grow.

Just don't stop there. You can meet them low, but make sure and take them high!

BUILDING KNOWLEDGE

In his article, "How Knowledge Powers Reading", educator Doug Lemov gives a great example of how prior knowledge impacts learning, maybe in ways we take for granted. He offers a long passage about a scene from a baseball game, using a lot of "baseball language". After reading it, you realize that if you happen to be a baseball fan, like I am, you fully understand the entire passage, but when you imagine reading it without a lot of prior knowledge about the game, you'd be lost.

When we think about prior knowledge, we usually think of younger students because their life experiences have limited their understanding of concepts adults take for granted. The longer you live, the more you experience, and the easier it is to make inferences that would otherwise be baffling. But think about the example I mentioned earlier; I'm a smart guy (and no spring chicken), but if that same passage were about fixing the transmission on a Mustang, I would be lost, regardless of my range of experiences.

Lemov points out in that same article that research identifies prior knowledge as having as much impact, and in some cases more, than traditional reading skills instruction when it comes to comprehension. Therefore, you have a definite instructional obligation to analyze texts and determine what gaps might exist in students' knowledge base that might impede their ability to comprehend the text. This might also include some academic language.

But you also have an opportunity. Creating lessons that ask students to research, inquire, or collaborate to investigate will certainly help close that knowledge gap and vastly improve comprehension. But it also opens new worlds to students, giving them new knowledge, and clears the way for them to not only understand but truly enjoy reading the text. And when we do that, we help build the kinds of minds that will continue to read, continue to inquire, continue to question, and continue to learn.

As I illustrated at the beginning, this knowledge gap applies to grown ups, too. So don't miss the chance to spark the minds of older students. And this can, and should, be a goal across the curriculum, driving engagement for all subjects and students.

As Dr Seuss said, "oh the places we'll go!" And you are how they'll get there!

SHARING A LESSON DISASTER

I am old enough to remember when teachers didn't all have PCs in their classrooms, and for a lot of us, we either typed lesson plans or handwrote them. Granted, that was the mid-90's, and by 2000, every teacher at least had a PC and access to a printer, and jump drives as well. But "back in the day", which was either a Monday or Friday, depending on who is telling the story, teachers didn't store everything on a hard drive.

I developed a phrase in my early teaching days because I quickly realized what it meant: "Beware the teacher who laminates her lesson plans." Basically, stay away from those teachers who were so sure of their teaching mastery that they had no plans to alternate their lessons from year to year. I found that those teachers were resistant to change, critical of feedback, and indifferent to collaboration, and their students tended to be behind students of other teachers at the beginning of the next school year.

The reality, and all teachers know this, even if some want to block it out, is we all make mistakes. We have all created and tried to implement a stinker of a lesson. We have all attempted an activity that was a disaster, or at best, a misfire. All of us. It's normal, especially as we are growing in our profession, or if we have changed schools, grade levels, or subjects. And administrators are just as prone to mistakes: strategies we thought would work, solutions that are not really solutions, actions we didn't fully think through. And ironically, we learn more from those miscues than from some of what we got in college.

I am always trying to find ways to make lemonade from lemons, and one way is to embrace that Lesson Disaster. Here is a strategy I have given to principals as a way to improve collaborative culture in a school, but you can do it with a partner, department, or grade level. During a planning meeting, everyone brings in a failed lesson or activity. It has to have already bombed, not just one that is incomplete. This is best done in groups of three or four, but could be done in pairs as well. With a partner or group, briefly describe - in 30 seconds -

that the lesson or activity is and what it tried to teach. Then in 60 seconds, describe how it bombed. Then exchange with a partner, or rotate with a group, and take turns silently making notes on your colleague's lesson, with suggestions - no criticisms. After all, the teacher already knows the lesson needs help, so don't rub salt in the wound. By the time everyone gets his or her lesson back, it has benefitted from another's expertise and can be revised for next time.

More than that, a new component to the working relationship has been established. Whether one is a seasoned veteran or a first year teacher, the understanding that no one is perfect but everyone can improve is created and strengthened. Moreover, a teamwork mentality is firmed up. And finally, the shame of not being perfect is shattered. Because we're not. The only mistake is thinking you don't make one and not learning from it.

TEACHING RESILIENCE:
FAILURE IS KEY TO SUCCESS

We all grow up hearing stories of successful people who initially failed but kept working until they succeeded. Some have almost become cliches: Abraham Lincoln losing several elections before winning; Thomas Edison and George Washington Carver watching experiment after experiment fail until they finally found the answers they were seeking, and with all of those individuals, their resilience and perseverance have impacted humanity on a global level. On a smaller scale, I love the story of basketball Hall of Famer Michael Jordan talk about getting cut as a 9th grader from his high school basketball team. Even he admitted he wasn't very good at the time, but he kept working and working until he made the team, and then went on to be a champion at every level.

Teachers and administrators tell me all the time that "kids today" simply don't have the resilience of generations before. They give up quickly or treat failure as an embarrassment and deterrent from trying again. They expect things quickly and correct, that with current technology, they have been conditioned to not stay on anything too long, that if it isn't working, they give up and move on.

I see it in schools as well. And the problem isn't always technology or apathy or the "Everyone gets a trophy" attitude in our society. Some of it comes from a real feeling that failure is a scarlet letter, that not succeeding is shameful. And when that feeling is present, resilience is non-existent.

But resilience and perseverance are key to succeeding in any endeavor. No one knows and can do everything. That's why we go to school - to learn what we don't know. And society doesn't always teach these qualities as organically as it did in decades past. Which is why it is so important that educators create schools and classrooms that make it OK to not know right away. To create environments where knowledge comes from learning from mistakes and failures. To make the "L" on the forehead mean "Learner" instead of "Loser" when students don't get something right on the first try.

How do you do that? There are several ways, and none of them involve purchasing a leadership or character program for thousands of dollars, and none of them will transform your classroom overnight.

First, as a part of your classroom management, never allow one student to make fun of another when contributing to class discussions, doing problems on the board, etc. That needs to be a non-negotiable, and if it persists, it warrants a parent call or conference.

Second, relate school to things in their own world. For example, most kids love video games. Ask them, "Why do you play the same game over and over again? Even when your player dies or doesn't save the princess or whatever, you keep playing - why? Do you get better each time you play?" We know the answer and so do they. Do the same thing with students who play sports or perform dance or play musical instruments. Why does the school's football coach watch film from the last game? Why do baseball players take batting practice every time they work out? Why does a musician keep trying to play the same song again and again? They are already displaying characteristics of resilience in their own lives; connect it to learning.

Also, and this is somewhat controversial, allow students to correct wrong answers on assignments, or allow retakes of failed tests. If you have the autonomy in your class to do that, I encourage it. The pushback I get from that is, "Life doesn't give you a retake. They need to learn to do their best, and if they know they can retake, they won't try." My first response to that is that it is not true; life is full of second chances, from retaking your driver's license test to things that at are deeper and more personal. Ask a teacher if s/he would want to live in a world where everyone had to be perfectly correct the first time, and they'd not only say "no", but they'd agree they have been the recipient of re-dos throughout their life. Further, ask yourself, "What is the purpose for me teaching a skill? For them to learn it or for me to assess it?" It's to learn, so if they are not getting it right away, allow them the struggle of working on it until it is right. Give partial credit instead of full on re-dos if you're concerned with equality in your grading, but give them the shot.

Finally, purposely make occasional small mistakes to see if they catch it, and when they do, own it and let them help you fix it. Remind them, as Thomas Hoerr states in *The Formative Five* that failure is a bruise, not a tattoo. And that it's OK to not know; it's not OK to not try. We learn from failure, better prepared to try again. All of us.

CONTROL

Every child deserves a champion—an adult who will never give up on them, who understands the power of connection and insists that they become the best that they can possibly be.

- Rita Pierson

Letting Go

What follows is a short five part series on control in your classroom. We will focus on what we can control, and what we cannot. How to move past what we cannot, and how he focus on what we can.

I'm not going to pretend this concept is easy. While I pride myself on not being a micromanager as a school administrator, lack of control has been a source of stress both in my life and in my career, so I am not speaking from the perspective of an expert but as a survivor. I still struggle with it, especially in traffic, so this is an ongoing journey. But I have found that when we focus more on what we do have control over, and make impact there, our frustration with that over which we have no control is lessened significantly. For example, I can't control the drivers in the cars around me, any more than I can control the road construction or fender-bender ahead of me. But maybe my frustration is because I am late, and more to the point, because I did not leave home in enough time to account for unexpected setbacks. THAT is in my control, so if getting to an appointment is really that important, I need to control what I can to make it happen, regardless of the things over which I have no control.

Now, let's make sure and define our terms here: by control, I mean absolute control. You may have a fabulous classroom behavior management plan in place and have no behavior issues in your class, but you don't *control* your students. You have influence over them, and you have found methods that encourage them to behave a certain way. They may love and respect you so that their desire to please you influences their good behavior. But make no mistake: you do not control them. There is no switch that turns them off and on, control dials that direct their moods and actions. We work in a business of people, and influence is all you can have over the thoughts, moods, attitudes, and actions of other people.

So control and influence are two different things. Here are some things you do NOT have control over in your job as a teacher: board policy, state regulations, federal funding, state allocations, the mandated core curriculum, what grade you teach, your children, their parents, your administrators, the weather, and any other acts of God. Wow, that's an extensive yet incomplete list. Makes you feel a little hopeless, probably. Just to turn the knife a little more, you don't have much *influence* over some of those things either. But as we discuss what you DO control in your job, you'll be able to let go of the stress of the lack of control in other areas.

Teaching is a job built on adaptation: throughout the centuries, teachers have integrated new learning, rolled with new ideas and influences, watched one set of students grow while welcoming a new, younger set, worked under different supervisors, mentors, principals, superintendents. We are used to making it work, so believe me when I say, you can do this!

ATTITUDE AND APPEARANCE

In discussing some things over which you DO have control, we're going to start by talking about attitude and appearance. Don't misunderstand what I mean by appearance: I don't mean society's version of beauty, so don't feel like you need to go to Glamour Shots. And with attitude, I don't mean "putting on a happy face" all the time.

I worked with a first year teacher who was having a rough year. Behavior management was an issue, and student engagement was almost non-evident. But what I also saw was how she allowed the stress of the job to affect her appearance. She started not washing her hair or, on some days, not wearing make up. And some days, she didn't even shower or wear clean clothes. She was clearly depressed, and luckily, some colleagues intervened and she got some counseling. But if we noticed that she had stopped caring through her appearance, so could her students, and this added to the classroom chaos. Look, I get it: there are some days when we are just faking it - we're stressed, tired, or the pressures of our non-work life start to creep in. I've been there, but if I let my outward appearance reflect my inner turmoil, I'm not sure if my unshaven, bed-head, body-odored self would be very effective as a teacher that day, and the belief that I didn't want to be there would not only not be evident but also influence student attitude as well. If I don't care, why would my students? And appearance goes a long way in showing how much you care, and it's something over which you have control.

Which brings us to attitude. Again, try to be positive at all times (have you ever noticed that the most negative teachers are rarely the good teachers?), but what I am really talking about is something I have mentioned in earlier chapters, and that is efficacy. John Hattie's meta-studies show that the second most impacting effect on student success is teacher belief in student achievement, just behind school/collective belief. This means that simply believing in students has an incredible positive effect on their success; that belief and how it is shown through your demeanor, actions, and words are all in your control. Think about that: within your classroom, you control the most powerful influence on student success, and it goes back to attitude. Do you exude confidence in your students? Do you communicate their importance? Do you inspire them to work harder? Do you help them individually achieve by treating each student as an individual? All of this is just attitude and what comes from it. You have control over this crucial element, which also means that a lack of this attitude could be devastating. It's like a superpower. Let's make sure we are using it for good!

QUALITY OF STUDENT WORK

I was heavily influenced by the work of the late Dr Phillip Schlechty during my teaching career, most notably his book, *Working on the Work*. It's a short book and a good read, and I highly recommend it, for teachers and administrators. The main focus of *Working on the Work* is the idea that of all of the things over which teachers do not have control when it comes to content, they do have control over the work they create for students. As a teacher, you do not have control over the curriculum. You may or may not have come control over a pacing guide or curriculum map, but in many cases, those were created by your school, system, or state. You don't control high stakes testing, and you work within a grading scale determined long before you arrived. But you control the quality of the work you give your students. You control the level of engagement, you control the level of rigor, you control the standards taught within. The complexity, the depth of knowledge, the legitimacy - all in your control. And when you create work that is authentically engaging, according to Schlechty, students will learn more, retain more, and apply this knowledge more. You control this.

As an English teacher, I enjoyed teaching the *Great Gatsby*, and it's a good thing, because I didn't have any choice. It was part of the 11th grade American Lit curriculum and mandated by my school system, so like it or not, I was going to be teaching it. But how I taught it was within my control. We could read the book (or I could read it aloud), take some quizzes, maybe a nice fat test at the end, maybe even a bubble-in test form so I could run them through the automatic grader during my prep period and have those grades done.

Or, we could explore the themes of wealth and power, of love and materialism. Maybe even have classroom debates on whether Daisy would be better off with Tom, Gatsby, or alone. Do a research paper, but let the students create topics and allow them choice. I could pose text-dependent questions that forced students to synthesize the knowledge from the novel into their own lives.

Or I could give a multiple choice quiz. Totally up to me. No, I didn't have control over what I taught, but I had control over how I taught it, and quality student work is the ultimate product of that control. I had the power to make the work authentically engaging.

But quality student work doesn't just happen; it involves quality planning, yet another way you control student success.

QUALITY OF PLANNING

Two quick analogies. I had a number of odd jobs while in high school and college, and at one point, I was a cook in a restaurant. One day, I had the prep shift, where I came in at 9AM even though we didn't start serving lunch until 11:30. I spent that time cooking and preparing certain things in advance so that when an order came back, we had the necessary preparation ready to make the quality meal in less than 15 minutes.

When I taught high school English, I was fanatical about my students creating tight and detailed outlines before starting a single draft of an essay. As I told them, if your outline is full of detail, the actual execution of writing the essay will be seamless because your thoughts are already fully organized. So it is with lesson planning.

Now I know you don't always have control over planning time at school. Impromptu parent meetings, scheduled data discussions, and other infringements on your planning time make it tough to guarantee that those times of the day when your students are with someone else will allow you time to plan. Even subject area or grade level planning meetings can become hijacked when others are involved. Whatever the situation, you have to make the time to plan well, whether it means shutting your door to nice but chatty co-workers, staying a little late after school one afternoon or coming in really early one morning, or possibly taking a little work home with you, you need to dedicate real time to do real planning.

Quality planning obviously connects to standards, and while you cannot control those, you can make sure they, along with data, are the driving forces of what you plan. We've discussed creating quality work, but that starts with truly understanding what you want students to learn. So quality planning also involves deep diving into a standard or learning outcome; analyzing texts, doing the math, breaking down the objectives.

Quality planning also involves anticipating where students might have difficulty, so control your lessons by being proactive with addressing possible learning obstacles, and plan for that so that instead of reacting to what they could not understand after the lesson is over, prepare them so that they have a better chance of understanding the first time. With planning, figure out how to connect the content to their lives or prior knowledge. Make the learning matter, and figure out how to engage each student. Make sure you plan for different learning levels and needs, but also plan with high standards in mind; just because this content may be new or students may not be at grade level yet, don't do them the disservice of leaving them low. Plan with those high expectations and rigor in mind. And finally, how will you internalize the lesson? How will you teach it confidently? All of these things are in your control. And all of these things will help create the kind of lessons that are easy to deliver but high impact.

FEEDBACK TO STUDENTS

How do we communicate with students? Now, obviously, you have control over your tone, volume, and word choice, and we mentioned that in a previous chapter about attitude. So yes, utilize control, even when you are frustrated or angry. And here again, I am telling you this as a survivor, not an expert. I have to work on that daily, so I get it.

But more to the point of today's discussion, I am talking more about the feedback you give students in regards to performance. We all want to know how we're doing, and while students may not be able to verbalize it as a coherent thought, all of them, from kindergarten to 12th grade, want to be pushed towards higher achievement, and all will view your interest in them as validation, even if on the inside you are thinking, "Well, that's my job." Feedback is an impacting way to do that. Whether you have individual conferences or simply call a student to your desk, feedback that leads to academic growth can have amazing effects.

With feedback, there a couple of characteristics that will make it successful. First, make it timely; a lot of students can't tell you what they did this morning, much less an assignment they did last week. Make it constructive; simply pointing out what went wrong or a student's current average in your class isn't leading towards improvement, just stating the status quo. This discussion should give students the belief they can grow academically. And make it specific; something like "If we can get a little more effort, I think your grade will come up" is encouraging, but it's too vague. Help provide strategies along with the encouragement.

These feedback opportunities give you a chance to make a huge difference. Feedback gives you a chance to increase student confidence and self-efficacy; by setting goals and showing that these goals ARE achievable, students internalize this and use it to succeed. Also, these conversations give you a chance to increase student responsibility; no longer is their achievement just a number on a test, report card, or spreadsheet. Their achievement has a face, and individual expectations have been created, which keeps students from hiding inside the anonymity of scores and grades. And with all of these factors, feedback increases student success.

I know that time is always an obstacle, especially at the secondary level where one teacher might have 150 students. So you will need to be creative with time and modes of communicating feedback. Spread your conversations out over several days if necessary. Or maybe focus your face-to-face discussions on your struggling students or those you know need a compassionate push. Or use notes to individual students, but if you do this, make sure you refer to a goal in an actual vocal communication at some point. For example, you may have given feedback notes to all students, and when the bell rings to end 3rd period and students are filing out, a casual, "Peter, I'm looking forward to seeing your progress on this week's project; tomorrow, I'll give you that resource I mentioned in my feedback, ok?" The point is to make it academic and unique to each student. The impact will be monumental, I assure you.

Special Days

Better than a thousand days of diligent study is one day with a great teacher.

- Japanese Proverb

(Author's note: these podcast episodes were delivered on specific days that tie the information therein to a particular occasion. They are no less enjoyable, but they are more specific.)

FIRST DAY OF SCHOOL

If it is not the first day of the new school year for you, it is definitely close, or in some cases, may have already happened. In any event, it is the season of renewal that comes with the beginning of a new school year.

Think about this: education, and teaching more specifically, may be the only profession in the world, outside of professional sports, where you get to start over every year. Obviously, many businesses and occupations work within fiscal or calendar years, and quarterly reports. But even then, it is just a demarcation, not a restart. Doctors can't start over every year with a new set of well patients. Banks don't annually empty the vaults and refresh their accounts with new patrons and investors. Construction firms don't finish all projects in May so that they can plan new buildings for August. I could go on, but you get the idea.

We get the opportunity to, after some refreshing, hit the reset button with a new set of children, new group of parents, a new collection of expectations and the opportunity to keep the successes from the previous year but get rid of the negatives, implement new ideas or maybe even improvements from mistakes we made the year before. Challenge ourselves in fresh, exciting ways.

And it is exactly that: an opportunity. A opportunity to look ahead with a fresh perspective. Maybe last year didn't reveal itself as a banner year; maybe you had an inordinately spirited homeroom; maybe you began a new job in a new school or maybe just a new grade level or subject; maybe you had "That" mom who seemed to have endless hours to make you aware of her concerns. And sure, you'll get a new set of adventures, but unlike our non-educator friends, we get a chance to start anew. So make the most of it and Good luck!

Best Year Ever? Why Not?

Every spring, my brothers and I take a trip to the Tampa area and experience spring training baseball. It combines our love of the national pastime and each other, our love of the Tampa area, and our love of our favorite teams (mine are the Phillies and Rays). Beautiful March weather when it's still winter everywhere else, salt air in the breeze, drenched in midday sunshine. And baseball. It really is one of my true happy places.

One of the beauties of spring training is the hope that permeates every game and crowd. The season hasn't started yet, so everyone is in first place! Maybe this is the year those off-season trades really pay off? Or maybe those young guys will emerge as stars? Or maybe the stars will all align with the moon, and a unicorn will deliver a World series ring, as a leprechaun rides on his back? Who knows? it could happen! The point is that before the season begins, and even in the first few weeks, it is possible for any team to believe this will be a special year.

For us in education, we also begin every year with new hope, a belief that this can be the best year ever. The difference is that we really can make that happen, a lot easier than the Rays winning the pennant. We have the tools within us to make this an amazing year, but so much of that is preparation and attitude. And are we setting the right expectations? So many times we strive for "perfection". But is that the best perspective? The truth is, there is no perfect teacher, no perfect student, and no perfect school year. We will have lessons that underperform, children who make mistakes, years with moments of frustration and stress. So why not focus on progress instead of perfection? Was last year less than your best, and how can you improve? Maybe it is a strategy, maybe it is a system you may or may not have in place, maybe it's knowledge you need to take your teaching to the next level.

We get to start each year knowing we have the realistic ability to make this year the best year ever, and unlike some teams who don't have what it takes to go all the way to the World Series, we all have the capacity to improve upon the year before and truly make this the best year.

The question is: will you do what it takes to make that happen? Everyone wants to be a winner, but not everyone *wants to do what it takes* to be a winner. So refocus, self-assess, and take the steps necessary to be better. A class full of kids is counting on it. And I know you can do it!

GIVING THANKS

In the next week, most schools across the country will be taking a week or so off in order to celebrate the Thanksgiving Holidays.

I really enjoy Thanksgiving, and not because of the fabulous food coma I will slip into by mid-afternoon on Thursday. I enjoy the family gathering and the time to recharge. But I also need Thanksgiving. I am guilty, like so many others, of allowing the speed, stress, obstacles, requirements, and distractions of life to keep me from accurately and adequately expressing thanks for all of the blessings I truly have. Thanksgiving grounds me, humbles me at times, but always fills my heart with the healing powers of gratitude.

Like you, I have many personal things for which I am thankful, but I will save those expressions for the ones who need to hear them. For today, I'm going to share some professional things for which I am thankful, and I hope some of these resonate with you as well.

I am thankful for a job that gives me the opportunity to make a positive difference in the lives of others. I know I may never see the true fruits of my labors, but I know the impact is real. Sometimes I question my occupational choice when I am feeling burned out, but in my heart of hearts, I know I am doing good every day I go to work.

I am thankful for the chance to grow and learn. I get to experience things that help me grow professionally and personally, and sometimes the teachers are the students. I get the chance to take that learning and use it to help others, and each year, I get the opportunity to hit the reset button and make my use of my skills and knowledge even better for students. And I get a chance to recover from those days I am not at my best to return the next day and make it right.

I am thankful for my colleagues. Do I get along with all of them? No. Most of them, yes, but it's impossible to like and connect with everyone, and I am sure I have colleagues who do not count David Seale as their favorite co-worker. But the vast majority of the people with whom I work are dedicated educators who inspire me to be better and support me in my own quest. And sometimes, they are just there for me when I need to whine or complain or celebrate, and I am just as thankful for that.

I am thankful I have a job. Period. As we get closer to the holiday season, I am reminded of those who will go without, and I am thankful I am able to provide for my family and enjoy comforts I sometimes take for granted. Even in times of job dissatisfaction, I am thankful for the employment in a field that serves others. I don't do it for a high salary, but I do do it for *some* salary, and that's just life. So I am thankful.

I am thankful for every child who has made me smile, laugh, or tear up with amazement or joy. Thankful for every success and moments of true progress, learning breakthroughs that show in the faces of students. Thankful for the bits of info I get from students who are now grown-ups themselves and leading full, productive lives.

And I am thankful I have the ability to take the time and express my thanks to those who mean so much to me. And I thank you and hope you find the five minutes we spend together twice a week meaningful in some way. My message to you today, if it isn't obvious by now, is that you, too, have been blessed, so take some time to count those blessings and thank those who help make them happen.

HOLIDAY STRESS

I hope everyone had a restful and meaningful Thanksgiving holidays. I have always been fond of Thanksgiving and view it as one of my favorite holidays, mainly because it asks us to take time and reflect on all for which we are thankful, and quite frankly, I need that. In fact, I ought to do that more often, because I am blessed and I have a lot for which to appreciate and humbly accept. And I'm not good at recognizing that like I know I should. I guess we are all guilty of that at times. It's easy to get caught up in the hectic business of life and take for granted the great things we have. So I hope you took some time to do that this past weekend, and I hope you got some good rest...

Because you're going to need it for these next couple of weeks leading up to the December holidays. For some reason, the weeks between Thanksgiving and the December holidays seem to be inordinately stressful. And in my time as an administrator in high poverty, low income schools, I noticed something bordering on a phenomenon. Bad behavior decisions increase tremendously during this short stretch. In fact, along with mid to late October, and mid-February, this time period represents one of the discipline spikes in a school year. And curiously, kids who are usually well-behaved, or at least manageable, will make bad behavior choices that are out of character for them. It can be frustrating as well as bewildering.

As I have owned before, I am not a psychologist or counselor by any means, but I have a theory in regards to this phenomenon. The holiday season tends to be very stressful for adults, as well, especially parents. Statistics show that the suicide rate in the US is higher in December than in any other month, and mixed with the "It's beginning to look a lot like Christmas" vibe, there is some real tension during this silly season. In other words, if our real lives were like "It's a Wonderful Life" most of us would identify more with the George Bailey standing on the bridge than the one gleefully shouting "Merry Christmas, Bedford Falls!" Take that holiday stress and apply it to parents from low-income homes. And then imagine how it trickles down to their children. Kids overhear mom and dad talking about a lean holiday this year, but have to hear some kid in their math class brag about the new video gaming system he's getting. They know that there isn't going to much under the tree again this year, but know they will see classmates with new expensive tennis shoes come January. The stress flows downward, and it is internalized by young people less equipped to process it. Which is why I think we see some good kids making uncharacteristically bad choices. Chances are, though, they don't know why they are talking back, being defiant, picking a fight, not doing homework.

I don't tell you this so that you feel compelled to buy every kid in your class a present, and sometimes, calling attention - any attention - to a perceived misfortune may make a child react negatively, so please proceed with caution in that respect. But I am asking for you to tap into that inexhaustible store of compassion you have in your heart. And exercise patience when you see kids behaving poorly. Obviously don't ignore it, but realize that something deeper may be going on that the child him or herself may not be able to verbalize, that the defiance may have nothing to do with you or school.

This time of the year often brings out the best in some people, in the form of giving and charity. But it can also cause stress, so as you think about those things for which you are thankful, count as one of them the opportunity to support your kids in a multitude of ways, when they might need it the most.

UNPLUGGING FOR THE HOLIDAYS

When I was working on my administrative degree, I had a professor state to the class, "There are no real emergencies in education." I wasn't quite sure what he meant at the time; most of the administrators I had worked for, especially at the central office, always seemed to indicate there was an emergency: "We must raise scores! We must implement this new thing, now! Why haven't you returned that parent's email? - she won't quit bothering me about it!" And I know people whose demeanor always seems to communicate that something is on fire, somewhere. You know the types. I avoid those types.

But as I moved into an administrative role, I slowly understood what he meant. There are no emergencies, just some urgencies. With any job, there are deadlines and expectations, some more urgent than others, and some that add pressure and increase stress, but emergencies? I have since amended my professor's statement to be a little more specific: Unless it involves a vehicle with a siren, there are no emergencies in education. That doesn't diminish the importance of our work, just puts it into perspective.

Which is why I told that story: to put some things into perspective as we move into the winter holiday season. Whether you celebrate a winter holiday or not, educators get a couple of weeks away from school, and the focus is usually on family and events. And of course, with New Years, most of us will go through the usually futile formality of making some type of Resolution for the year. However you spend your time off, you will get a chance to relax and recharge.

But only if you allow yourself to. Teachers are notorious for spending out-of-school time on school work, of keeping late hours to finish, to drag papers to grade to their child's ball game or dance lesson, to spend weekends planning, and they do it in the name of the students, which is very noble. Except that you are no good to your students if you are burned out and exhausted. Being an education martyr isn't doing anyone any good, even if you feel like you must keep working, and even if you can easily justify it by saying, "It's for the kids." You can't be your best if you don't take time to recharge. The fact is, you can't recharge until you first unplug.

One of my teacher friends works with a department whose members are notorious for evening and weekend group texts to discuss work issues. She said that it was impossible to unplug when colleagues wouldn't let her. I get this all the time. Either coworkers or parents think that you are on call, 24/7. You are not. There are no emergencies in education, I promise. You need the weekends, you need your evenings. You need your holidays. And others need you, and I don't mean your students. I mean family, friends. And *you* need you.

So how do you unplug?

First, inform colleagues that you are unavailable to communicate in the evenings, or at least on the weekends. Establish those boundaries, and suggest your department or grade level team find a way to have these discussions during the work day, or after the students leave. If you feel uncomfortable saying this for fear of hurting some feelings, simply don't respond to texts or emails when you are "off the clock". Trust me, they will get the hint. And inform parents at the beginning of the year that, like them, you spend your weekends with family and may not respond to weekend communications until Monday. Again, if they still insist on communicating on Saturday afternoon, don't respond. Once you do, you've opened the door and given them the indication that you are on call. Resist! There are no emergencies in education, even if people want to act like there are.

Along those lines, do a time audit of your time at work. Are there ways you could be more productive when you don't have children in your room that will allow you to accomplish more and leave work at work?

Most of all, put the important things first. With your time away from work, don't let work get in your head space and push out those meaningful things. I was having a discussion with some central office colleagues the other day, and one was talking about how her job was requiring her to work late almost every night. Another colleagued echoed something I have heard before but always need to hear again: The school system can replace you tomorrow if you go; your family never can. Further, make your time off restful as well as meaningful. Spend it doing things not related to work. And don't feel guilty about sleeping in every once in a while or having some YOU time. Clearly, some weekend and evening time has to spent doing laundry, buying groceries, cutting the lawn, etc., and I know that there are those times when you do need to grade a few papers or stay late. But explore some things you want to do as well as need to do.

So enjoy your time off! Unplug, then recharge, and come back into the new year and semester rested and ready to do the vital work you were born to do.

ABOUT THE AUTHOR

David Seale is the creator and host of the podcast, *Teacher Affirmations* and a career educator, with twenty-five years and counting in the profession. As a classroom teacher, basketball and debate coach, assistant principal, principal, and central office coordinator, his career has spanned grades K-12, with twenty of those years in Title 1 schools and/or systems. David is currently an Instructional Coordinator in the Birmingham City School system where he works with administrators and teachers in fifteen schools across the city.

He also performs music for kids at public libraries across the region as Capn Dave; you can find his albums of original children's music on iTunes, Amazon, and other digital music outlets. Further, he writes and records music for grown-ups, too, so look him up on those same sites. And no, none of the songs are about teaching. We all need creative diversions, David included.

Bibliography

Blankstein, A. M. (2004). Failure is not an option: Six principles that guide student achievement in high-performing schools. Thousand Oaks, Calif: Corwin Press.

Hattie, J. (2012). Visible learning for teachers: Maximizing impact on learning.

Lemov, Doug (Feb 2017) **How Knowledge Powers Reading** Educational Leadership, v74 n5 p10-16

Schlechty, P. C. (2002). Working on the work: An action plan for teachers, principals, and superintendents. San Francisco: Jossey-Bass.

Sinek, S. (2009). Start with why: How great leaders inspire everyone to take action. New York, N.Y.: Portfolio.

Whitaker, T. (2012). What great teachers do differently: Seventeen things that matter most. Larchmont, NY: Eye on Education.

Whitaker, T., Breaux, A. L., & Ebook Library. (2013). The ten-minute inservice: 40 quick training sessions that build teacher effectiveness.